Mrs.Brown

Jorge Consuegra

EXT. THE GROUNDS OF WINDSOR CASTLE, FOREST - NIGHT
Begin on black. The sound of rain driving into trees.
Something wipes frame and we are suddenly hurtling through a forest on the houlders
of a wild-eyed, kilted JOHN BROWN. Drenched hair streaming, head swivelling left
and right, as he searches the lightening-dark. A crack to his left. He spins round, raises
his pistol, smacks past saplings and plunges on.

EXT. THE GROUNDS OF WINDSOR CASTLE, FOREST - NIGHT
Close-up on BROWN as he bangs against a tree and heaves for air. A face in its fifties,
mad-fierce eyes, handsome, bruised lips, liverish. He goes on searching the dark.
Stops. Listens through the rain. A beat. Thinking he hears a faint thump in the distance,
he swings round and races on.

EXT. THE GROUNDS OF WINDSOR CASTLE, FOREST - NIGHT
BROWN tears through the trees, pistol raised at full arm's length, breath coming harder
and harder. But even now there's a ghost grace, a born hunter's grace. He leaps fallen
branches, swerves through turns in the path, eyes forward, never stumbling once.

EXT. THE GROUNDS OF WINDSOR CASTLE, FOREST - NIGHT
BROWN bursts into a clearing, breaks to the centre and stops. With his pistol raised,
he turns one full slow circle. His eyes take in every swerve and kick of the wildly
swaying trees.
There's a crack and a branch snaps behind him. He spins round, bellows deep from his
heart:

BROWN
God save the Queen!!
And fires.
Nothing happens. The trees go on swaying, the storm goes on screaming and BROWN
just stands there, staring into empty space. A pause.
Slowly, he starts to frown as the fact begins to dawn on him that he is alone. He stares
at the thrashing trees, waving their mocking arms at him. His hand lets the pistol drop
to his side. He feels the rain drench down his face.
And now, for the first time, we see that his socks have fallen to his ankles and his knees
are cut to shreds. He shifts a foot. His dress-shoes are covered in mud. He goes on
staring into the dark. Nothing.
Just the wind and rain. Gradually, we pull back, higher and higher. As we do, we hear
the quiet cultivated voice:

FADE TO BLACK.
CAPTION: "1864"
FADE IN:
PONSONBY (V.O.)
I have sent for a Mr. John BROWN from Balmoral. Her majesty has mentioned him,
on one or two occasions, as being a most devoted outdoor servant to Prince Albert
during his last days there...

John BROWN is now just a tiny figure dwarfed by the storm.

CUT TO:
INT. OSBORNE HOUSE, QUEEN VICTORIA'S DRESSING ROOM - DAY
The screen is black. As the camera pulls back, we discover that we are looking at a black night-gown.
Queen VICTORIA is sitting at her dressing table, while an elderly HAIRDRESSER, also in black, works at her hair.

PONSONBY (V.O.)
... The depths of the Queen's sorrow remain impenetrable. She has now restricted herself to a regime of such ferocious introspection that we are all at our wits' end...

INT. OSBORNE HOUSE, PRINCE ALBERT'S DRESSING ROOM - DAY
A bust of the Prince Consort is draped in black. His desk is laid out as if for work. A VALET is brushing one of his suits before laying it carefully on the bed.

PONSONBY (V.O.)
... The Household continues, at her instruction, to observe the rituals now so familiar to her, in a vain attempt to render vivid that which can never be revived...
Close-up on a small table as a shaving brush is placed carefully beside a dish of freshly poured water.

INT. OSBORNE HOUSE, QUEEN VICTORIA'S DRESSING ROOM - DAY
The hairdresser is pulling VICTORIA's hair back into the widow's cape. For the first time, we see her face. It is set in a mask of severity.

PONSONBY (V.O.)
... It will not surprise you to hear that she continues steadfast in her refusal to accept any public engagements, however trivial...

INT. OSBORNE HOUSE, QUEEN VICTORIA'S BEDCHAMBER - DAY
A bronze cast of Prince Albert's hand hangs above the Royal bed. His sleeping-gown is laid out on one side.
A somberly dressed middle-aged man stands by the bed:
DOCTOR JENNER, the Queen's physician. He is placing potions and medicaments in a row on the bedside table.
Behind him, TWO MAIDSERVANTS are busy stripping and remaking the bed while another raises the window to air the room.

PONSONBY (V.O.)
... Family and staff expend all their efforts endeavouring to draw her out of this state of unfettered morbidity, but to no avail. Indeed, Doctor Jenner will not undertake to vouchsafe her sanity, unless some remedy is found...

INT. OSBORNE HOUSE, QUEEN VICTORIA'S DRESSING ROOM - DAY

VICTORIA is turning slowly around as a young ASSISTANT DRESSER completes the fastening on her black crepe dress.

PONSONBY (V.O.)
... We must hope, therefore, that this Mr Brown will appeal to the Queen's sentimental, though deeply-held, view that all Highlanders are good for the health. If she can at least be persuaded to take the air, the prospect of further recovery may seem less remote...
The assistant dresser pulls too tightly on her dress.
VICTORIA winces slightly.

ASSISTANT DRESSER
(terrified)
Sorry, ma'am.

EXT. THE SEA FRONT, ISLE OF WIGHT - DAY
We glide slowly past the coastline as a caption reads:

"ISLE OF WIGHT. 1864."
A DRIVER stands against the sea front with a horse and cart bearing the Royal coat of arms.
John BROWN leads his pony along the dockside, towards the waiting driver. He is in his late thirties, fit, handsome and dressed in tartan kilt and short jacket.

PONSONBY (V.O.)
... He is arriving by boat this afternoon, by which time it is hoped
Her Majesty will be in a fit state to consider riding out...

INT. OSBORNE HOUSE, PRIVATE SECRETARY'S ROOM - DAY
SIR HENRY PONSONBY, the Queen's Private Secretary, is sitting at his writing desk, completing a letter.

PONSONBY (V.O.)
... As to that decision, along with all others, we remain, as ever, prisoners of the Queen's grief.
(beat)
Ever your devoted husband, Henry.
He folds the letter and slips it into an envelope. He is a middle-aged man in a dark mourning suit; tall, Saturnine and with a civil servant's stoop. As he looks up, we see a white-stockinged FOOTMAN standing to attention by the door.
PONSONBY hands the letter to him.

PONSONBY (CONT'D)
Windsor.

CUT TO:
CAPTION: "OSBORNE HOUSE, ISLE OF WIGHT"

INT. OSBORNE HOUSE, CORRIDOR AND QUEEN'S DINING ROOM - DAY
A series of windows are being slammed open by white stockinged FOOTMEN as members of the ROYAL FAMILY and UPPER HOUSEHOLD hurry by in silence, all dressed in mourning and rushing to make the luncheon hour.

INT. OSBORNE HOUSE, QUEEN'S DRAWING ROOM - DAY
Queen VICTORIA heads down the empty corridor with two ladies-in-waiting, LADY ELY and LADY CHURCHILL, hurrying along a pace behind.

INT. OSBORNE HOUSE, QUEEN'S DINING ROOM - DAY
Members of the Royal family and upper household hurry into the icy dining room and take their designated places at the luncheon table. Everybody is dressed in mourning and nobody speaks. Wind whistles through the open windows.
Silence.
Among the diners we catch our first glimpse of BERTIE, the
Prince of Wales. He is in his mid-twenties, plump, stiff dressed and balding. He stands next to his young wife, PRINCESS ALEXANDRA, who fiddles nervously with her shawl, trying to keep warm.
As BERTIE smooths down his thinning hair, DOCTOR JENNER bustles into the dining room, stands himself next to PONSONBY and proceeds to conduct a hurried conversation with the Prince of Wales, entirely in whispers.

JENNER
Congratulations, Your Royal Highness!

BERTIE
Thank you, Doctor.

JENNER
A boy, I hear. Excellent, excellent.

BERTIE
Yes.
(beat)
Albert Victor. Eddie for short. What do you think?

PONSONBY
A fine choice, sir.

JENNER
Excellent!

EXT. DOCKSIDE, ISLE OF WIGHT - DAY
JOHN BROWN leads his pony gently up the ramp and into the carrier bearing the Royal coat of arms. The DRIVER leans in.

DRIVER
Are you riding up front?
BROWN looks straight at this man, quiet and reserved.

BROWN
I'll stay with the pony, thank you.
She's all the way from Deeside and she's not sure she likes you yet.
The DRIVER shrugs and slams the doors on them.

INT. OSBORNE HOUSE, CORRIDOR AND QUEEN'S DINING ROOM - DAY
VICTORIA reaches the dining room door and takes a deep breath. LADY ELY and
LADY CHURCHILL stop a pace behind.

VICTORIA
How many?
LADY ELY is slightly taken aback.

LADY ELY
The Royal Family and senior members of the household, ma'am.

VICTORIA
Just them?

LADY ELY
Yes, ma'am.
VICTORIA closes her eyes, then steels herself and steps through the door.

INT. OSBORNE HOUSE, QUEEN'S DINING ROOM - DAY
Everyone stiffens as VICTORIA walks in. Acknowledging the other diners with a
quick nod, the Queen takes her place.
She flaps open her napkin and, bang on cue, everyone else sits and does the same. The
meal is served immediately by waiting SERVANTS, who plonk the food down without
ceremony.
It's a very ordinary meal of meat and vegetables. VICTORIA starts eating heartily,
straight away. Everyone does the same.
Only the clink of cutlery and the same eerie silence.

EXT. OSBORNE HOUSE, THE GROUNDS - DAY
The Royal horse-carrier rattles into the grounds and on down the driveway past the
beautiful, manicured lawns stretching away towards the ornate twin towers of Osborne
House. A few outdoor servants watch its progress curiously.

INT. OSBORNE HOUSE, QUEEN'S DINING ROOM - DAY
The silence continues as VICTORIA finishes her plain pudding. Immediately, servants
appear at every place and whip away the pudding bowls whether their owners have

finished or not. Nobody thinks this odd; it is part of the routine. DOCTOR JENNER clears his throat.

JENNER
We're expecting Brown this afternoon, ma'am.

VICTORIA
Whom?
A beat. VICTORIA takes a sip of water, dabs her mouth with her napkin and rises. Everyone else rises too. Suddenly, the Queen turns to Bertie's nervous wife, PRINCESS ALEXANDRA, and proclaims abruptly:

VICTORIA (CONT'D)
That's a very pretty shawl you are wearing, Alex. Silk suits you well.
(beat)
But you are not eating enough. One must not let vanity overrule one's appetite.

PRINCESS ALEXANDRA
Yes, ma'am.
VICTORIA nods earnestly. Lost to the effect her words have had, she marches out again. Behind her, she leaves PRINCESS ALEXANDRA feeling humiliated and crestfallen in front of all the others. BERTIE takes her hand and squeezes tight, trying awkwardly to console.

EXT. OSBORNE HOUSE - DAY
The horse-carrier pulls up outside the servant's entrance and the DRIVER opens the doors.
JOHN BROWN pulls out a watch from his waistcoat and checks the time. His eyes narrow critically.

BROWN
I was due at a quarter past one.
(beat)
You're late.

INT. OSBORNE HOUSE, CORRIDOR - DAY
A few minutes later, JOHN BROWN strides down the long corridor with PONSONBY at his side. Their journey takes them down an endless series of corridors, past servants and householders hurrying about their duties. The presence of the dead Albert is felt all around in the black-wreathed portraits and busts that crop up along the way.
BROWN and PONSONBY could not be more contrasted.

PONSONBY
(in low tones)
Her Majesty's routine at Osborne House is not as you will remember it. The Household remains in full mourning and no-one is permitted to raise their voice under any

circumstances whatsoever. As for the Queen's routine, she breakfasts at nine thirty, lunches at two,takes tea at five thirty and dinner at eight forty five. No one is allowed to leave the building while the Queen is at home.

On the rare occasions when she is out, you may ask permission to leave, but only with my consent.

You're to be ready to walk the pony at any time after ten o'clock. You'll clean her outdoor things and do any odd jobs as and when she requires.

BROWN
How will I know?

PONSONBY
(surprised to be interrupted)
I'm sorry?

BROWN
How will I know what she requires?

PONSONBY
You'll be sent a message.

BROWN
Who'll bring it to me?

PONSONBY
Her Highness' Equerry.

BROWN
I need a man who knows where I am.

PONSONBY
I'm sure it won't be difficult to find you.

BROWN
That's not good enough.
A beat.

PONSONBY
Then we'll have to see what can be arranged.

BROWN
Aye, do.
PONSONBY stiffens. A beat.

PONSONBY

There is to be no communication with other members of the household on matters concerning the court except through myself or one of the Equerries. No plans must be altered unless you are given prior authority by myself or a senior member of the household.

BROWN
I came down at the Queen's request.
I'll take my orders from her.

PONSONBY
In matters concerning the Household, I act on her behalf.
BROWN takes the measure of him.

BROWN
Do you?

PONSONBY
Yes.
(beat)
I do.
BROWN glances up the corridor.

BROWN
So, is passing wind out of the question or do I need permission for that?
PONSONBY refuses to acknowledge what he has heard. They reach the door of the Royal Chamber and he concludes the interview.

PONSONBY
As I am sure you remember from
Balmoral, you do not talk while in Her Majesty's presence unless Her Majesty addresses you directly.
BROWN refuses to answer, so PONSONBY knocks. After a moment, the door is opened by LADY ELY who ushers them in.

INT. OSBORNE HOUSE, QUEEN'S SITTING ROOM - DAY
BROWN walks stiffly into the room and stops. PONSONBY waits by the door.

PONSONBY (O.S.)
Mr Brown, ma'am.
VICTORIA is bent over the desk, working at one of her numerous red boxes. She scribbles furiously at a letter, underlining and accenting words as she goes. Finally, LADY ELY steps up to her side and whispers something in her ear.
She carries on working.
BROWN has time to survey the room. Dominating everything are the same black-wreathed busts and portraits of Prince Albert glimpsed in the corridor.
Finally, VICTORIA nods and LADY ELY beckons BROWN forward.

He steps up in front of the desk and waits. VICTORIA looks up and BROWN bows deeply.
Silence.
She stares at him for a long moment without apparently registering who he is. He towers over her, in bright tartan, while she sits hunched in her seat, all in black and knotted with tension.
Finally, she finds her voice. She sounds nervous and edgy.

VICTORIA
Mr Brown.

BROWN
Ma'am.

VICTORIA
You are here safely.

BROWN
Aye, ma'am.

VICTORIA
You are well?

BROWN
I am.

VICTORIA
And the pony?

BROWN
She's well, too.
VICTORIA blinks at the sight of him. His presence is bringing him back. A beat.

VICTORIA
Your family sent cards. It was much appreciated.

BROWN
I'm glad of it.
In an effort to control her emotions, VICTORIA now sounds the same severe note as at lunch. But BROWN, unlike others, seems unaffected.

VICTORIA
My husband was always very complimentary in speaking of you. He would have approved, I am sure, of my calling on you in this way.
(beat)
I trust it does not inconvenience you too much.

BROWN
I've no family, ma'am, apart from my brothers and sisters.

VICTORIA
Yes.
(beat)
You have a brother in service here, do you not?
(furrowing her brow)
I forget his name.

BROWN
Archie.

VICTORIA
Yes.
(beat)
That will be company for you.

BROWN
Yes, ma'am.
Silence. VICTORIA starts to tire. She takes a sip of water and spills a little on herself. Flustered, she searches for a hanky but cannot find one. LADY ELY hurries up with one of her own and the Queen dabs it off. BROWN watches all of this with genuine concern. When VICTORIA finally looks up, he stares at her in deep sympathy.

BROWN (CONT'D)
Honest to God, I never thought to see you in such a state. You must miss him dreadfully.
VICTORIA stares back in stunned silence. PONSONBY coughs involuntarily. LADY ELY freezes. A beat.

VICTORIA
You do not - he ... get him out.
(beat)
Get him out. Get him out!
Suddenly, BROWN finds himself tugged backwards out of the room. LADY ELY rushes up to assist as VICTORIA shouts herself into a fit of uncontrolled sobbing.

INT. OSBORNE HOUSE, BROWN'S QUARTERS - DAY
Some minutes later, BROWN is angrily unpacking a trunk.
His humiliation expresses itself in the extraordinary ferocity with which he slams down every object.
His younger brother, ARCHIE, sits on the bed. He's in his early thirties, bright, sharp and dressed in the same distinctive kilt and tweed.

ARCHIE

(telling it fast)
So the day they arrive, she greets the
Sultan and his family with barely a word and then retires to her chamber.
The Sultan, not used to State
Occasions without a head of State, is standing in the lobby waiting for someone to tell him what to do. But the court is under strict instructions not to talk in the corridors so nobody speaks to him, not a living soul, for the whole afternoon. So now it's dinner and everyone's standing round the table -- still not a word -- waiting for Her Majesty to arrive.
One hour goes by, two, the Sultan's getting a wee bit peckish to say the least. So finally, his wee laddy breaks for the cold meats and stuffs a slice in his mouth. Well, the uproar when she heard. You'd have thought someone had stolen the crown jewels.
BROWN stares back, still pissed off.

BROWN
So?

ARCHIE
So, there are rules. Things you do and things you don't do.

BROWN
I was just telling the woman how I feel, for God's sake.

ARCHIE
You don't tell Her Majesty how you feel.

BROWN
I speak as I find, Archie.

ARCHIE
Not down south you don't.
BROWN slams a drawer shut. ARCHIE lets it go and watches his brother. A beat.

ARCHIE (CONT'D)
So what did Ponsonby do when she started shouting?

BROWN
I think he nearly ruptured his truss.
A beat, then both men burst out laughing.

INT. OSBORNE HOUSE, SERVANT'S HALL - DAY
The clatter of voices and banging doors as under servants hurry about with plates, knives and forks, laying the Upper
Servant's huge table for dinner. ARCHIE leads BROWN through this rush of activity.

BROWN

How much?

ARCHIE
Seventy a year.

BROWN
Not bad, not bad.

ARCHIE
How about yourself?

BROWN
Sixty.

ARCHIE
(grinning)
That's pretty good for a ghillie.
BROWN smiles dryly. They pour themselves a drink from the table.

BROWN
Prince Leopold? Is he the one who bleeds all day? So what does his valet do? Wash his poultices for him?

ARCHIE
It's better than shovelling horse shit.

BROWN
If you were looking for promotion, you should have picked one of the healthier ones.

ARCHIE
She's hardly a full hamper herself.

BROWN
(beat)
It's only grief makes her like she is.

ARCHIE
Three years, John. Is that not a bit long to be grieving?

BROWN
She loved him.

ARCHIE
Come on, man. There's love and there's ...

BROWN

What?

ARCHIE
You know what I mean.

BROWN
I'm not sure I do, Archie.

ARCHIE
There's love and there's behaving like you do because there's nobody to tell you not to.
Hold on BROWN. He lets it go and moves on. Across the hall, he spots the pretty
ASSISTANT DRESSER watching them.

BROWN
Which one of us is she flirting with?

ARCHIE
The good-looking one.

BROWN
Aye? Then she's obviously not got enough to do.

ARCHIE
You work the system right, you could ask her yourself. Just be thankful you're not
working for Household. The
Queen never lets them out of her sight. But wee spats like us can slip through the net,
easy.
A beat. BROWN stares straight at him.

BROWN
I'm no wee spat, ARCHIE.

INT. OSBORNE HOUSE, UPPER CORRIDOR - MORNING
The next day, VICTORIA and her ladies are hurrying down a corridor on her way into
the dining room. VICTORIA suddenly stops and stares out of the windows. Her
entourage are several steps past her before they realize what's happened and scurry back
to take up their positions behind.
Now we see what has caught her attention. BROWN is standing in the courtyard below,
by his pony. She watches him for a moment, then without reacting, walks on.

EXT. OSBORNE HOUSE - AFTERNOON
Some hours later. It is now raining.
A gaggle of ROYAL GRANDCHILDREN hurry out of a carriage from their afternoon
recreational while their NANNIES frantically try to keep them dry under the umbrellas.
John

BROWN stands tall and erect on the gravel while they rush around him, laughing and giggling.

INT. OSBORNE HOUSE, UPPER CORRIDOR - EVENING
Rain on the window. VICTORIA is walking in the opposite direction down the corridor with her entourage. She stops at the same place as before.

VICTORIA
(as if she had not seem him earlier)
Who is that?
Lady Ely peers through the rain.

LADY ELY
It's Mr Brown, ma'am.

VICTORIA
What is he doing there?

LADY ELY
He appears to be ... standing by his horse.

VICTORIA
I made no request to go out riding today.
(beat)
How long has he been there?

LADY ELY
I don't know, ma'am.
(nervously)
He was observed earlier, I believe.
At this moment, PONSONBY comes down the corridor.

VICTORIA
Sir Henry, Mr Brown is standing in the courtyard. I have no wish to go riding.

PONSONBY
I'm very sorry, ma'am. I can't imagine -- he was certainly given no instructions.

VICTORIA
Please make sure it does not happen again.

PONSONBY
Of course, at once.
VICTORIA takes one last look and walks away.

INT. OSBORNE HOUSE, PRIVATE SECRETARY'S CHAMBERS - NIGHT

Half an hour later, PONSONBY stands at his desk facing

BROWN.
PONSONBY
What on earth did you think you were doing?
BROWN stares straight back.

BROWN
Awaiting my orders.

PONSONBY
You do not report for duty unless the
Queen requests it. You know that very well.

BROWN
I didn't come all this way to sit on my arse.

PONSONBY
You will await your orders like everyone else. Unless you prefer a repeat of yesterday's little excitement.

BROWN
No.

PONSONBY
I beg your pardon?

INT. OSBORNE HOUSE, UPPER CORRIDOR - DAY
The next day. From a high window, we see PONSONBY scuttling madly across the courtyard towards the figure of
JOHN BROWN, who is standing exactly as he was the day before.
VICTORIA watches impassively.

EXT. OSBORNE HOUSE, COURTYARD - DAY
PONSONBY stands close to BROWN, shouting in his face.

PONSONBY
I thought I made myself perfectly clear. You do not leave your room until Her Majesty requests it.

BROWN
(eyes straight ahead, shouting back)
Well, you tell Her Majesty from me, if her husband was here now, he'd have had her out of that house and getting some air in her. What the hell's the point in me being here otherwise?!

From the window above, VICTORIA takes in his words. A beat. PONSONBY collects himself.

PONSONBY
Go inside at once.

BROWN
Is that the Queen's request?

PONSONBY
Yes, it most certainly is!
BROWN turns, grabs the lead rein and leads his horse back to the stables.

INT. OSBORNE HOUSE, STABLES - DAY
A few minutes later, BROWN is in the process of stabling his horse. Suddenly he turns. VICTORIA is standing at the far end of the stable with her entourage.

VICTORIA
Mr Brown.

BROWN
Yes, ma'am.

VICTORIA
You have been told repeatedly not to stand in the courtyard unless requested to do so.

BROWN
Yes, ma'am.

VICTORIA
Then why do you persist in doing it?

BROWN
Because I think Her Majesty is wrong.
If ever there was a poor soul who needed fresh air, it is her.
A beat.

VICTORIA
The Queen will ride out if and when she chooses.

BROWN
And I intend to be there when she's ready.
Silence. The two of them stare at each other.

EXT. OSBORNE HOUSE, THE GROUNDS - DAY

The next day, high and wide over the stunningly manicured landscape. Long lawns, wind-cropped copses and in the distance, the glittering sea.

EXT. OSBORNE HOUSE, THE GROUNDS - DAY
VICTORIA sits side-saddle on a horse. BROWN leads her in silence.

EXT. CLIFFTOP - DAY
VICTORIA looks up.

VICTORIA
Prince Albert was going to build a bench here. He thought it one of the best views in Osborne.

BROWN
It's a fine spot, ma'am.

VICTORIA
He thought so, yes.
She stares ahead.

VICTORIA (CONT'D)
In everything I do and everything I say, I try to think, as much as possible, what he would do, or say, if he were here now. My Private
Secretary wishes me to return to public duties--
She stops abruptly, but BROWN cuts in.

BROWN
If Prince Albert were here today, he'd tell him a thing or two.

VICTORIA
Sir Henry is not alone. They all wish it.
(beat)
The same people who refused to grant my husband the title of King because he was deemed of insufficient rank--
She stops again, cutting quickly back to small-talk.

VICTORIA (CONT'D)
It is a fine spot for a bench, is it not?

BROWN
Aye, ma'am.

VICTORIA
Yes.
A pause.

VICTORIA (CONT'D)
I have some letters in the saddle bag.
I wish to read them.
BROWN walks up to her side, opens the saddle bag and hands her a bundle of letters
held together with ribbon.

VICTORIA (CONT'D)
I cannot read them like that.
BROWN undoes the ribbon and tries again. VICTORIA cuts in.

VICTORIA (CONT'D)
You will hand them to me as I require.
BROWN takes off the top letter and hands it to her.

INT. OSBORNE HOUSE, UPPER SERVANT'S TABLE - NIGHT
The clatter and crush of the Upper Servant's table as UPPER
SERVANTS sit themselves down to dinner while UNDER SERVANTS prepare to
serve soup.
ARCHIE comes in and sits himself somewhere in the middle next to an empty seat. A
moment later, BROWN strides in.
But instead of sitting at the place beside his brother, he goes straight to the head of the
table and plonks himself down. Slowly, the clatter dies away as the whole room stops
and stares at him in silence. BROWN fixes them with a look.
An elderly butler steps into the room and stares in amazement at BROWN. A smooth
young man, BERTIE'S VALET, hurries up to intercede.

BERTIE'S VALET
Mr. Carter, the Head Butler, sits there.

BROWN
Not now he doesn't. This is my place.

BERTIE'S VALET
By whose authority?

BROWN
My own.
A little frisson of oh-my-gawdness. BERTIE'S VALET stares icily at him.

BERTIE'S VALET
The order of seating at the Upper
Servant's table is arranged personally by the Queen herself.

BROWN
That's a tautology lad.
(unable to stop himself seriously explaining it)

If you say the Queen arranges something, you've no need to say she's done it personally. That's understood.

But as far as BERTIE'S VALET is concerned, it isn't. He stares down in mute fury, then snaps his fingers at one of the under servants, who rushes over. There is a hurried exchange of whispers before the under servant rushes out.

Unperturbed, BROWN brings out his flask and pours himself a substantial draft of whiskey. He turns to the pretty assistant dresser, sitting to his right.

BROWN (CONT'D)
Are you dresser to Her Majesty?
She blinks nervously at him.

ASSISTANT DRESSER
Assistant, sir, yes.
BROWN tucks into his soup. Everyone watches and waits.

BROWN
What's your name?

ASSISTANT DRESSER
Mary Taylor, sir.

BROWN
Have I seen you up in Balmoral, Mary?

ASSISTANT DRESSER
I hope to go up next year.

BROWN
You wouldn't happen to know what the
Queen's reading for recreation, would you, Mary?
The assistant dresser thinks for a moment.

ASSISTANT DRESSER
Lord Tennyson, sir?
BROWN nods. All conversation stops as the under servant bursts back in. She halts at the door, looking blankly from Bertie's valet to the elderly butler. A beat. The old man stiffens and makes his way to the middle of the table.
BROWN looks up from his soup.

BROWN
Am I the only one eating?
With a clatter of spoons, everyone obediently eats.

INT. OSBORNE HOUSE, DRAWING ROOM - DAY

A few days later. A morning "drawing room." Standing round the unlit fireplace are
DOCTOR JENNER, LADY ELY, LADY
CHURCHILL, the two LADIES IN WAITING and PRINCESS
ALEXANDRA. All are dressed against the icy wind that whistles through the open
window where VICTORIA sits knitting busily while BERTIE stands beside her, coat
buttoned up to the collar. PONSONBY has stationed himself opposite, beside a desk
piled high with red dispatch boxes.
He runs through the daily itinerary.

PONSONBY
Lord Clarendon arrives, by invitation, at eleven o'clock, followed at twelve by a picnic
in the grounds to celebrate Princess Alice's birthday.
Dispatches, as usual, at two.
(finishes, then coughs)
The Chancellor writes to say that, by happy coincidence, he will be in Cowes for the
weekend. He asks if Your
Majesty might grant him an audience.

VICTORIA
Why?

PONSONBY
He thought, perhaps, Your Majesty might wish to be informed of the latest
developments in government.

VICTORIA
No. I shall be out walking.
A beat. BERTIE watches closely now. PONSONBY coughs again, nervous.

PONSONBY
Then perhaps Your Majesty might consider it opportune if the Prince of
Wales were to meet him on your behalf?
VICTORIA stiffens. She speaks without turning.

VICTORIA
On no account.
PONSONBY gives up. Politely, but firmly, BERTIE takes up the reins.

BERTIE
Mama, I really do think it's time we made ourselves a little more ... available.
VICTORIA carries on knitting.

BERTIE (CONT'D)
I think we must accept our position in the country is not entirely unrelated to the
continued absence of the
Monarchy from public life.

(silence)
I thought perhaps we might consider a small gesture of some kind?
VICTORIA looks up sharply.

VICTORIA
Gesture?

BERTIE
I thought, a dinner for our ambassadors perhaps?

VICTORIA
(cutting in firmly)
No dinners, Bertie.
(beat)
Why are you dressed for outdoors?

BERTIE
It's so infernally cold in here.

VICTORIA
Cold is good--
(calling across)
Is that not so, Dr. Jenner?!

JENNER
I'm sorry, ma'am?

VICTORIA
Cold is good!

JENNER
Excellent, ma'am, excellent.
(trying his hand)
But perhaps if her Majesty were to consider accompanying her new-found physical vigor with the benefits of mental activity...

VICTORIA
(becoming very agitated)
Why am I being lectured in this way?!

JENNER
Forgive me, Your Majesty. In no way did I wish to suggest--

VICTORIA
(cutting across him)
I will not tolerate anybody lecturing me about the responsibility of the monarchy....

BERTIE
Mother....

VICTORIA
... Least of all my son. It was his irresponsibility that drove my husband to his grave.
An appalled silence. With great dignity, BERTIE absorbs the shock of the insult and
quietly steers the conversation in another direction.

BERTIE
If it is inconvenient to Her Majesty, then perhaps she might consider allowing the Prince
of Wales to host--

VICTORIA
I do believe they send so many boxes to taunt me.
Doctor Jenner writes to them to say that my nerves are in an extremely fragile state and
yet they continue to hound me with box after box after box after box after box!
Silence. VICTORIA has crossed to the window and stares out at the view. Having
recovered her composure, she turns to address them all.

VICTORIA (CONT'D)
I wish to take the Princesses for a swim.
For a moment, nobody believes what they have heard. She continues.

VICTORIA (CONT'D)
The turns I have been taking in the grounds have proved most beneficial to me, and
Brown thinks that salt water will do me good.
Bertie stares at her in silence while PONSONBY and DOCTOR
JENNER exchange a worried look.

EXT. PRIVATE BEACH, ISLE OF WIGHT - DAY
The doors of the Royal bathing-machine swing open and Queen
VICTORIA, in a voluminous swim-dress, sails out like a duck into the freezing sea. As
she does so, the doors of the other machines open and Princess Helena and Princess
Louise follow her in. Dignity does not allow them to shout out, but their expressions
of constipated agony are a picture.
VICTORIA begins swimming around in a vigorous little circle.

VICTORIA
Don't potter, children. Swim.
Hold for a moment on the princesses' miserable faces.

EXT. OSBORNE HOUSE - DAY
Half an hour later, PONSONBY, DOCTOR JENNER, LADY ELY and two
FOOTMEN watch as BROWN helps VICTORIA up some steps and onto her horse.
He glances at the stiff line of householders and mutters curtly to himself.

BROWN
You could buy that lot for garden ornaments and still see change from ten guineas.
The household do not hear this, but QUEEN VICTORIA has overheard and tries to suppress a smile.
As she settles into the saddle, her foot comes loose.
BROWN fastens it into the stirrups.

BROWN (CONT'D)
Lift your foot, woman.
Everyone hears this. VICTORIA obeys. Taking the reins, he then walks the QUEEN out of the courtyard. As they vanish from site, we hear...

DISRAELI (O.S.)
This nation is fortunate in so much as it is not governed by force...

FADE TO BLACK.
CAPTION: "1866"
FADE IN:
INT. THE HOUSES OF PARLIAMENT - DAY
The speech continues as we follow the progress of a
Tomahawk cartoon doing the rounds of the Tory back benches from knee to knee. It is entitled, "Where is Britannia?" and shows an empty throne draped with the Royal cloak.

DISRAELI (O.S.)
... but by a chain of traditions that have been cherished from generation to generation, because in them -- in our traditions -- are embodied all the laws which have enabled us to create the greatest empire of modern times...
During the above, the cartoon reaches the front benches and lands on the knees of the young, earnest STANLEY. As he frowns at the picture in front of him, DISRAELI winds up.

DISRAELI (CONT'D)
... but, even though we have amassed great capital and even though we have established an industry with no parallel in the world, yet all these mighty creations are as nothing compared to the invisible customs that shape our lives. To those honorable gentlemen of the opposition who seek to destroy the essential elements of this country, I say let them remember:
England cannot begin again.
During this peroration, we see DISRAELI for the first time.
He is handsome, obviously Jewish and wire thin, like
Dickens on Slimfast. He dresses almost dandyishly but speaks with startling vigor; a combination of brilliance and cheek that is his key. To cheers from his back benchers, he sits.
As he looks up, he catches the eye of his opposite on the

Liberal benches. GLADSTONE is different in almost every respect; dour, dogged, heavy-set and tall. They stare levelly for a second, then DISRAELI flashes a brilliant smile.
STANLEY plops the cartoon on his lap.

STANLEY
Have you seen this?

INT. THE HOUSES OF PARLIAMENT, LOBBY CORRIDOR - DAY
A few minutes later, DISRAELI and STANLEY are strolling down the busy lobby corridor. Throughout their talk, Tory back-benchers bustle up to pat their hero on the back and offer their congratulations.

STANLEY
Should we take it seriously?

DISRAELI
The cartoon or Her Majesty's absenteeism?

STANLEY
Well, both.

DISRAELI
The question is, do we need her?

STANLEY
Surely, you're not suggesting we dispense--

DISRAELI
My dear Stanley, a Prime Minister with only a handful of friends must respect public opinion.
The pass GLADSTONE in a huddle of cohorts.

DISRAELI (CONT'D)
Gossip counts. Lord Aberdeen was right. This country is not governed by wisdom but by talk.
(beat)
Granted, it wouldn't take much to winkle the old girl out of mourning, but if public opinion is against her, then it doesn't do to appear too close.

STANLEY
So?

DISRAELI
We'll see which way the wind blows.
DISRAELI sweeps through a prattle of back-benchers.

25

EXT. PUBLIC BEACH, ISLE OF WIGHT - DAY
BROWN and ARCHIE crash into the water. It is freezing.
BROWN braces himself against the icy shallows by bellowing
Burns at the sea.

BROWN

My heart's in the Highlands, my heart is not here! My heart's in the
Highlands a-chasing the deer! Chasing the wild deer and following the roe!
My heart's in the Highlands wherever I go!
ARCHIE is so creased up with laughing, he almost drowns.

EXT. PUBLIC BEACH, ISLE OF WIGHT - DAY
A few minutes later, BROWN and ARCHIE hurry back up the cold beach to rub
themselves dry. BROWN is very energized.

BROWN

One box of biscuits, one box of drop tablets, one box of pralines, sixteen chocolate
sponges. It's the same order every week, but does anybody bother to check it? Now
she has to travel all the way to Balmoral without the few luxuries she actually enjoys.

ARCHIE

So? Someone'll send it on ahead.

BROWN

Aye, but will they?

ARCHIE

John, it's not your problem what she eats.

BROWN

The woman's surrounded by fools!
(beat)
She has to be packed and ready to leave by seven thirty tomorrow morning. Knowing
that lot, they'll still be dressing her at eight.
BROWN takes a nip of whiskey and offers some to his brother.

ARCHIE

She's got an army of people to get her up and out.

BROWN

But I'm the only one she trusts.
ARCHIE stares at him. A beat.

ARCHIE

She'll blow hot and cold on you, John, she always does. You want to be careful.

BROWN
I'm on ninety pounds a year plus seventy pounds for a pile of tartan
I'd be wearing anyway. That's as much as a Page of the Back Stairs gets and that job's
only for toffs.
(raising his hip flask triumphantly at the sea)
I'm Her Majesty's Highland Servant!
Indoors and Out. There's no stopping me now.

EXT. BALMORAL CASTLE - NIGHT
A few days later.
The clatter of carriage and horse as the ROYAL PARTY thunders through gathering
dark toward Balmoral Castle.

CAPTION: "BALMORAL"
EXT. BALMORAL CASTLE - TWILIGHT
A mass of torches encircle the ROYAL PARTY as kilted
GHILLIES and STAFF swarm round the carriage, opening doors and clambering off
boxes while a regiment of PIPERS play them in.
Amid this swarm of activity, we glimpse BROWN opening the door to a smiling
VICTORIA as she climbs down, followed by
PRINCESS HELENA and PRINCESS LOUISE. Emerging from another carriage
come BERTIE and PRINCESS ALEXANDRA, staring grim faced at the castle.
HENRY PONSONBY and DOCTOR JENNER alight from their carriage as
PONSONBY slips on his gloves and pinches his nose at the pain of remembrance.

PONSONBY
Oh God, not the pipes!

EXT. LOCHNAGER - DAY
The next day.
High over the vast, bleak mountains of Lochnager and Loch
Muick. VICTORIA and BROWN are riding fast towards the top.
Reaching the summit, VICTORIA points excitedly at the far horizon.

VICTORIA
What are those?

BROWN
What?

VICTORIA
Those, over there, there.

BROWN
(horse chestnut trees...)

Craobhan-geanmchno-fhiadhaich.

VICTORIA
(beat)
Craobhan-geanmchno...
(bursts out laughing)
How can I possibly say that with a straight face?!
BROWN lets it go and they ride on.

VICTORIA (CONT'D)
I am thinking of publishing my
"Highland Journals."

BROWN
Are they worth reading?

VICTORIA
(beat)
I am told so.

BROWN
Who by?

VICTORIA
Sir Henry Ponsonby tells me they are charming.

BROWN
What does he know about the Highlands?

VICTORIA
He has been attending at Balmoral for many years.

BROWN
That doesn't make him an expert.

VICTORIA
His remarks were directed at the quality of the writing, not its subject.

BROWN
I don't groom a horse to have it admired by others, I groom it because it needs grooming.

VICTORIA
(curtly)
I do not do it for others. But
Ponsonby thinks they are good.

BROWN
Just say what you have to say, woman.
What other people think shouldn't matter to you.

VICTORIA
(snapping)
Of course I shall say what I have to say. I always do.
The stare at each other until BROWN kicks his horse on.

BROWN
Aye, well, if all you want is a good opinion then he'd be sure to oblige you.

VICTORIA
(riding alongside)
What Mr Ponsonby was appreciating was their literary merit, a skill not intimately associated with the knowledge of grooming.
(beat)
Literary appreciation does not begin and end with Tennyson.
BROWN lowers his head.

VICTORIA (CONT'D)
(in a softer tone)
I mention you in them.
BROWN says nothing.

VICTORIA (CONT'D)
In particular, the occasion when
Albert was alive; the Royal Carriage overturned during a storm and you demonstrated such loyal service in returning the Queen and the Princesses safely to Balmoral.
Taking a sprig of heather from her brooch, VICTORIA holds it out to him. A beat.

VICTORIA (CONT'D)
For friendship.

INT. BALMORAL CASTLE - DAY
A few days later, PONSONBY, DOCTOR JENNER and BROWN stand at the chamber-desk, talking over the Queen's itinerary.

BROWN
(briskly)
She'll be away on Friday between eight o'clock and six in the evening to visit the Grants in Glasalt. If she's to make the journey there and back in the day she's to have no distractions the night before. She'll take a light supper alone in her private drawing room and retire early.

PONSONBY

She'll need to sign dispatches before she retires.

BROWN
That can wait till the weekend.

PONSONBY
There are important papers from --

BROWN
It can wait. Anything else?

JENNER
Are you sure Her Majesty is up to such a long journey? She has only just recovered from a severe head cold.

BROWN
If I thought she wasn't up to it, I wouldn't let her go, would I?
BROWN snaps together his papers and walks out, leaving
PONSONBY and DOCTOR JENNER standing lamely at the table.

EXT. BALMORAL CASTLE - DAY
The next morning. The ROYAL FAMILY are picnicking in the grounds. VICTORIA walks along a path accompanied on one side by BROWN, on the other by BERTIE. BERTIE is in mid-plea.

BERTIE
Surely it is for the gentlemen to decide when to stop...

VICTORIA
It is a disgusting habit, Bertie. It should be discouraged.

BERTIE
Yes, but isn't midnight a little excessive?

VICTORIA
It is quite late enough.

BERTIE
But mama, the room was built expressly for that purpose. It has been a smoking-room by tradition ever since father --

VICTORIA
(cutting in angrily)
Brown's responsibilities are onerous enough already. He has far too much to do without having to stay up all night waiting for you to go to bed.
The smoking-room will be closed and the lights put out at twelve o'clock.

BERTIE
Mama...

VICTORIA
And that is my last word on the matter.

BERTIE
Well, I'm sorry, but I really do think it's too much that the gentlemen of the house should be dictated to by a servant.

BROWN
It's the Queen's decision.

BERTIE
I beg your pardon?
(to VICTORIA)
Mama...?
Before Bertie can continue, BROWN steps right into his face.

BROWN
I think you should go now.
(beat)
You've tired your mother enough.
BERTIE stares back, too stunned to speak. He glances at his mother, but VICTORIA looks off into the distance as if she has not heard. BERTIE turns and storms away.

INT. ESTATE COTTAGE, BALMORAL - DAY
JOHN BROWN is standing in the doorway of a small cottage watching, with amused detachment, as a middle-aged couple,
MR and MRS GRANT, race about their tiny living room, trying desperately to make it presentable for the Queen's sudden visit. They fling open the windows, slosh water on the fire, tidy up their two grubby BOYS, plump up the cushions, dump knitting under the sofa and try to smarten themselves up, all in the space of a few seconds.

BROWN
There's really no need for this.

MRS GRANT
I'll not have her seeing it like it is!
(beat)
I know she means well, but I wish she'd warn us she was coming.

BROWN
She thinks if she warned you, you'd go pouring water on the fire and stuffing the knitting under the sofa.

MR GRANT
Aye, well, you can't stop a wife being house-proud.
MRS GRANT surveys the room critically.

MRS GRANT
All right.
(beat)
Show her in.

EXT. ESTATE COTTAGE, BALMORAL - DAY
VICTORIA sits on a horse and trap. BROWN steps out and helps her down.

BROWN
They're ready now.

VICTORIA
I hope they didn't go to any trouble,
John.

BROWN
Ah, well...

INT. ESTATE COTTAGE, BALMORAL - DAY
VICTORIA steps in to be greeted by all four GRANTS in one military row, smoke still
steaming off the fire. BROWN stands behind her, barely able to contain himself. But
for
VICTORIA, it is all she's ever known and so she takes it as perfectly normal.

VICTORIA
Mr Grant. How good it is to see you.

MR GRANT
(bowing deeply)
Your Majesty.

VICTORIA
Mrs Grant. How is your knee? Has the pain eased a little?

MRS GRANT
(bobbing in terror)
Oh not so bad, ma'am.

VICTORIA
Good. Oh and here are Douglas and
John. Haven't you grown?

MRS GRANT
(still bobbing away)
Growing all the time, ma'am.
MR GRANT remembers himself and gestures VICTORIA towards a chair.

MR GRANT
Will you sit, ma'am?
From his place by the wall, BROWN notices how easily she smiles as she is led to the chair. She points to a picture on the wall and her good humour is infectious.

VICTORIA
I know that! That's Cairn Lochan. We picnicked there once, did we not, John?

INT. A SOCIETY PARTY, LONDON - DAY
A few days later, a party of ARISTOCRATS, MINISTERS, DIPLOMATS, ESCORTS, BUSINESSMAN and WHORES. Into this brouhaha come DISRAELI, his elderly wife MARY ANNE and the young STANLEY. It is all eyes and nods here. Everyone knows everyone.

DISRAELI
Ah, the greasy pole.

MARY ANNE
Don't be facetious, dear. Remember your position.

DISRAELI
It's my position I'm thinking of.
Across the room, STANLEY spots BERTIE amid a crowd of acolytes.

STANLEY
I see the Prince of Wales is here.

DISRAELI
I hope he got his mother's permission.
STANLEY smiles faintly. DISRAELI homes in on a punter and raises his hand, already working the room.

DISRAELI (CONT'D)
Lord Salisbury!

INT. A SOCIETY PARTY, LONDON - DAY
The society party is hotting up. STANLEY is deep in conversation with three SOCIETY LADIES.

SOCIETY LADY 1
(ridiculously pleased with herself)
Why is the Queen penny-wise and pound foolish? Because she looks after the
Browns and lets the sovereigns take care of themselves!
A peal of naughty laughter. Unseen, DISRAELI steps up.

DISRAELI
And in your opinion? Is she foolish?
The SOCIETY LADY stares blankly back.

SOCIETY LADY 1
Well I ... well, I mean to say, it's hardly right, is it?

DISRAELI
What?

SOCIETY LADY 1
Well, the Queen and --
(appalled whisper)
Mr Brown.
DISRAELI stares at her steadily, already thinking ahead.

DISRAELI
La superstition met le monde entier en flammes.

SOCIETY LADY 2
(thick as shit)
I beg your pardon?

DISRAELI
(changing tack)
Has anybody seen this ... Mr Brown?

STANLEY
He is her personal servant, I believe.

SOCIETY LADY 1
(knowingly)
Follows her wherever she goes.

DISRAELI
He would hardly make a very good personal assistant if he did not.

INT. ESTATE COTTAGE, BALMORAL - DAY
BROWN stands by a wall, smiling to himself at the sight of
QUEEN VICTORIA struggling to help lay the table while MRS

GRANT nervously prattles on.

MRS GRANT
... it's not my best china. I mean, it is my best china now, but the family set got stolen last summer.

VICTORIA
Oh, I'm so sorry ...

MRS GRANT
Of course it was no-one on the Estate.
More likely one of the lads from
Braemar. Or further even.
(beat)
I'll fetch the salt.
MRS GRANT scurries away. VICTORIA immediately holds up the spoons to BROWN with a questioning look -- above or beside the plate? He nods her to the top and she quickly carries on.

INT. A SOCIETY PARTY, LONDON - DAY
DISRAELI and MARY ANNE stand with BERTIE and his ACOLYTES.

BERTIE
Mr Disraeli. Ma'am.

DISRAELI
Your Royal Highness. What a pleasure to see you here.

BERTIE
Have you met Mr Lyle? He's in sugar...?

DISRAELI
I don't think I've had that pleasure.
DISRAELI shakes hands with the fat sugar tycoon who wobbles with drink. MARY ANNE engages him in conversation while
BERTIE turns DISRAELI aside.

BERTIE
No doubt you've heard the rumors.

DISRAELI
I take no account of gossip, Your
Highness.

BERTIE
My concern is for the reputation of the Monarchy.

DISRAELI
Of course.

BERTIE
I fear the influence he has on her.
The man's word is not to be credited.
He is an arriviste of the very lowest water.
(beat)
She's having a bust cast of him. In
Nero Marquino marble.

DISRAELI
I see.

BERTIE
I would talk to her myself, but she won't listen to me. She must be persuaded, by someone she respects, to abandon this ridiculous favoritism before a situation develops.

DISRAELI
A situation?

BERTIE
I don't imagine you frequent the
Republican Clubs. But the fact that neither you nor I are members should not blind us to the significance of their existence.
(beat)
The Tory Party has always been our party.

DISRAELI
I'm flattered you think so.

BERTIE
I tell you, if we don't stick together on this, you could find yourself First
President's Opposition.
(murdering it)
Du Royaum Uni.

DISRAELI
Quite.
A beat.

BERTIE
I don't think we can overstate the seriousness of this.
DISRAELI nods and BERTIE walks swiftly back to his party.
The moment he's gone, STANLEY steps up to DISRAELI's side.

STANLEY
What did he want?

DISRAELI
To know when he'll be king.

INT. ESTATE COTTAGE, BALMORAL - DAY
VICTORIA, BROWN and the GRANTS are eating around a large table. Like a wife watching her husband, VICTORIA beams proudly at BROWN as he tells a story.

BROWN
... so Grant here and myself are riding over Lochnagar and the rain's pouring down in sheets and all we're thinking about is getting home for a drink, when through the gloom Grant spots a couple of poachers. He gives me a shout and we chase them down towards the loch until Grant has your men up against the stacks and he's shouting and cursing at them, "Why are you poaching on Royal land?!" And one of the little fellas looks up at him and says, "coz we've come up in the world."
For a split second, both the GRANTS look petrified, then
BROWN and VICTORIA explode into laughter and the GRANTS relax. Suddenly the GRANTS are helpless with laughter too.
Beginning with VICTORIA's glass, BROWN pours out liberal quantities of whiskey all round.

EXT. BALMORAL CASTLE - DUSK
Later that night, the courtyard is packed with a gaggle of worried HOUSEHOLDERS holding lamps.
Through the light, BROWN and VICTORIA clatter into the courtyard on the horse and trap. DOCTOR JENNER breaks through the crowd in a state of high excitement.

JENNER
Your Majesty! Thank goodness you're safe! I'll have a bath prepared immediately. I recommend Macdonald's
African Embrocation --

BROWN
(cutting in)
Ah, pipe down, man. The woman's fine.

VICTORIA
We stayed a little longer than expected with Mr and Mrs Grant. It was most agreeable.

PONSONBY
We were expecting you to return by six.

VICTORIA

And now I am back.
BROWN cannot resist one more little dig.

BROWN
We took a nip of whiskey.

VICTORIA
To keep out the cold.

BROWN
Aye.
VICTORIA smiles and BROWN lifts her off the trap. Before walking in she turns and, in front of everyone, says...

VICTORIA
Thank you, John.
BROWN bows and the QUEEN walks on. As she straightens up, he finds PONSONBY and DOCTOR JENNER staring back at him in utter disbelief at what she has just said. He turns and leads the horse back to the stables.

JENNER
(under his breath)
She's drunk.
PONSONBY doesn't answer. He is watching BROWN very closely.

JENNER (CONT'D)
A distinct flushing around the cheeks.
She was drunk, I tell you.

PONSONBY
No, she wasn't.
Silence. JENNER turns to look at PONSONBY.

JENNER
Surely not ...
PONSONBY's face is set hard.

PONSONBY
Don't even think about it.

INT. BALMORAL CASTLE, BALLROOM - NIGHT
A crush of kilted GHILLIES as we slam into the height of the annual Ghillie's Ball. The whole court is reeling through the dance; all of them beholding the extraordinary spectacle of QUEEN VICTORIA and
JOHN BROWN dancing together in the middle of the hall.

PONSONBY and JENNER stand by the wall, watching. Close-up on PONSONBY'S face as JENNER mutters darkly.

JENNER
Pandora's Box ...
With a slam of feet the reel ends, the GHILLIES roar and
BROWN and VICTORIA stand smiling at each other in silence.
A King and his Queen.

INT. BALMORAL CASTLE, BALLROOM - NIGHT
Later that night.
We find BROWN, slouched on the ground, dead-drunk and snoring loudly.

EXT. LOCHNAGER - DAY
A few days later, four JOURNALISTS are scrabbling up a stony path, armed with telescopes.

EXT. LOCHNAGER - DAY
A large ROYAL PARTY is making its way smoothly and quietly up the mountain.
BROWN is on horseback, leading VICTORIA on a dapple-grey.

EXT. LOCHNAGER - DAY
The JOURNALISTS rattle up the hill.

EXT. LOCHNAGER - DAY
BROWN and VICTORIA start pulling ahead of the main party.

EXT. LOCHNAGER - DAY
The JOURNALISTS scramble up to some gorse bushes, dump themselves down and start setting up the telescopes.

EXT. LOCHNAGER - DAY
BROWN and VICTORIA near the summit when BROWN suddenly stops. He stiffens and turns to face the wind, as if catching a scent. VICTORIA frowns.

VICTORIA
What is it, John?
(beat)
John?

BROWN
I heard something.
BROWN's eyes fix on some distant gorse bushes.

BROWN (CONT'D)
I won't be long.

He dismounts and races off.

EXT. LOCHNAGER - DAY
The JOURNALISTS are peering through their telescopes.

JOURNALIST 1
Where did he get to? I've lost him?
Below them, BROWN races across the riverbank and undergrowth, unseen.

JOURNALIST 2
I don't know if there's much worth writing about.

JOURNALIST 1
Hard to tell.
BROWN rears up above them and stops.

BROWN
This close enough for you? Go on! On your way! You filthy scavengers!
The JOURNALISTS scramble to their feet and start legging it down the hill, while BROWN roars furiously, hurling their bags after them.

BROWN (CONT'D)
You leave her alone, do you hear?!
The JOURNALISTS vanish below the hillside.

INT. BALMORAL CASTLE, UPPER SERVANT'S TABLE - NIGHT
That night.
BROWN is standing at the head of the table, yelling at the
UPPER SERVANTS, irrespective of ARCHIE or anyone.

BROWN
If I catch the miserable by-blow who told those men where she'd be, then
I'll hang his balls to dry on Jock
Wemyss, so I will!!
ARCHIE glances up at BERTIE'S VALET. He is staring down at the table, teeth gritted, fists clenched. BROWN rounds on them all again.

BROWN (CONT'D)
What happens to John Brown is his business, but the Queen's security will never be compromised!

BERTIE'S VALET
We --

BROWN
You'll talk when I'm finished!

BERTIE'S VALET stares at him in astonishment. BROWN turns back to the table.

BROWN (CONT'D)
That kind of disloyalty will not be tolerated in this house, is that clear?
(beat, yelling)
I said, is that clear?!
There is a general mutter of assent. BROWN turns and storms out as ARCHIE gets up to follow.

INT. BALMORAL CASTLE, HENRY PONSONBY'S ROOMS - DAY
A few days later, PONSONBY is sitting at his desk, hands to his hips, listening quietly as DOCTOR JENNER reads from his copy of Punch.

JENNER
"Court Circular, Balmoral."
(beat)
"On Tuesday, Mr John Brown enjoyed a display of sheep-dipping by local farmers. On Wednesday, he attended a seance where he was pleased to listen to a recital of Auld Lang Syne by Mr
Robert Burns himself ..."

INT. BALMORAL CASTLE, LOWER CORRIDOR - DAY
BROWN crashes through a door holding a copy of the same journal.

JENNER (O.S.)
"... On Thursday, Mr John Brown walked on the slopes, accompanied by family and friend ..."

INT. BALMORAL CASTLE, CORRIDOR - DAY
BROWN storms up to PONSONBY's door.

JENNER (O.S.)
Mr Brown retired early.

INT. BALMORAL CASTLE, HENRY PONSONBY'S ROOMS - DAY
BROWN bursts in on PONSONBY and JENNER, slamming down his copy of Punch on the desk. He is furious but controlled.

BROWN
If I find out that you had anything to do with this, I will have you sacked.

PONSONBY
I believe that decision rests with Her
Majesty.

BROWN

Don't think I can't persuade her.

PONSONBY
I don't doubt that the Queen was highly amused. She has always had a very healthy sense of humor.

BROWN
This is a slur on her good name.

PONSONBY
In as much as the article is about yourself, I think you must now accept that the public has a right to its interest in you.

BROWN
Nobody has any rights over me.

PONSONBY
We are all of us subject to forces beyond our control, Mr Brown, even you.
BROWN stares at him in silence. A beat.

BROWN
You'll regret saying that.

FADE TO BLACK.
CAPTION: "1867"
FADE IN:
INT. THE HOUSES OF PARLIAMENT - DAY
Chaos. The Tories are losing the vote as both sides of the house stand and shout at each other while the SPEAKER rises in his chair.

SPEAKER (O.S.)
Order! Order! ORDER!
A buzzing silence settles as the house sits for the vote.
The COUNTERS approach the chair.

SPEAKER (CONT'D)
Result of the vote to the first reading of the Bill to Disestablish the Irish Church.
A murmur of excitement from the LIBERALS.

SPEAKER (CONT'D)
Order!
A beat.

COUNTER
Ayes to the right, three hundred and thirty, noes to the left, two hundred and sixty-five...

By the time he reaches "sixty-five" his voice is drowned in cheers from the Liberal benches. DISRAELI and the rest of the front bench sit in stony silence.

Somewhere on the Liberal back benches, a wild-eyed maverick, DILKE, rises to his feet shouting:

DILKE
Mr Speaker, I table a motion in furtherance of the Bill to
Disestablish the Monarchy!
A roar from the irate TORIES and chaos reigns again.

SPEAKER
Order! Order!! ORDER!!!

INT. THE HOUSES OF PARLIAMENT, LOBBY CORRIDOR - NIGHT
An hour later the house is empty except for a few straggling MPs hurrying home. An exhausted DISRAELI stands in the corridor with STANLEY.

DISRAELI
We're going to lose.

STANLEY
You can't know that for sure.

DISRAELI
Gladstone's got his party facing the same way for the first time in years.
We need help.
(long beat)
Where is the old girl?

STANLEY
Who?

DISRAELI
Mrs Brown.

STANLEY
It's questionable whether there's any advantage to be had from that direction. She's never been less popular.

DISRAELI
In the press, perhaps.
(holding up Punch)
But she's sold more copies of her
Highland Journal in three months than
Punch will ever sell in a year. Time to wheel her out.

STANLEY
She's refusing to leave Balmoral.

DISRAELI
What's her excuse this time?

STANLEY
The Princess Louisa is too ill to move. Frankly, the Queen's rather upset at the recent spate of bad publicity.
(beat)
You're smiling.

DISRAELI
I was trying to imagine "rather upset."
The elderly prelate, DEAN WELLSELLY, hurries in through the lobby doors. DISRAELI puts on a welcoming smile.

DEAN WELLSELLY
Forgive me, gentlemen. I'm late.

DISRAELI
Not at all, Dean. Good of you to spare the time.

DEAN WELLSELLY
I came as quickly as I could.

DISRAELI
You've seen the latest cartoon in
Punch, I take it?

DEAN WELLSELLY
(completely lost)
I beg your pardon?
DISRAELI opens the copy of Punch and hands it to Dean
Wellselly. The Dean clears his throat and starts to read.

DISRAELI
(as Wellselly reads)
One of our madder brethren in the house was calling for disestablishment of the monarchy.
Dean Wellselly looks up from the article, horrified.

DEAN WELLSELLY
Good Lord.

STANLEY

(playing the soft glove)
I'm sure it won't come to that.

DISRAELI
(the hard glove)
No. But it has now become a matter for our consciences.
(beat)
I was just telling Stanley how vital it is that the nation should feel the visible influence of the Sovereign.
As a reminder that Parliament, indeed my own ministry, depends on the will of the Queen.
DEAN WELLSELLY nods his head gravely. Over his shoulder,
STANLEY is gaping at DISRAELI's silky distortion of the party political maneuver into a moral imperative.

DEAN WELLSELLY
I couldn't agree with you more, but I am only Dean of Windsor. I don't understand what ...
DISRAELI interrupts.

DISRAELI
We hear from Balmoral that Mr Brown is interesting Her Majesty in some of the forms of worship associated with ... low-church Presbyterian.
Silence. DEAN WELLSELLY'S face is a picture of unrestrained horror. Low-church. Presbyterian.

DEAN WELLSELLY
What can we do?

DISRAELI
Oh, several things.

INT. BALMORAL CASTLE, QUEEN'S DRAWING ROOM - DAY
Some days later.
Queen VICTORIA sits at her desk while Henry PONSONBY stands in front of her, holding a copy of The Times.

VICTORIA
Read it.

PONSONBY
Again?

VICTORIA
Read it!
PONSONBY coughs once and begins again.

45

PONSONBY

"The Times wishes to join the rest of
Her Majesty's loyal subjects in expressing its deep joy at the news that the Queen is soon to come out of her mourning."
VICTORIA glowers at him.

VICTORIA

Who told them that?

PONSONBY

I have no idea.

VICTORIA

Why not?

PONSONBY

I -- forgive me, ma'am, I am no wiser than yourself.
Suddenly, VICTORIA's temper goes and she shouts at him.

VICTORIA

No-one should think themselves wiser than me!
(beat)
It is not for any of the Queen's subjects to presume to tell Her
Majesty when and where She should come out of mourning. It is the Queen's sorrow that keeps her secluded! It is
Her overwhelming amount of work and responsibility, work which She feels will soon wear her out entirely!

PONSONBY

Your Majesty --

VICTORIA

(cutting right through him)
Is it not enough that She is uncheered and unguided that she should also have to suffer these malicious rumors?!
(a pause, more quietly)
I am not a fool.
(beat)
I know there are those in the establishment too afraid to attack me and so they attack my dearest friends.
Sometimes -- I feel that Brown is all
I have left of Albert.
(beat)
And now they attack Brown too.
She looks up, eyes blazing.

VICTORIA (CONT'D)
I will not give him up to them.

INT. BALMORAL CASTLE, ROOM ADJOINING DRAWING ROOM - DAY
BROWN is guarding the door to the drawing room while the balding BERTIE muscles up, eye ball to eye ball.

BERTIE
I wish to see my mother.

BROWN
She's busy.

BERTIE
Convey her a message.

BROWN
She's away to Windsor tomorrow. Talk to her there.

BERTIE
Tell her the Prince of Wales wishes to speak with her urgently about matters concerning the press.

BROWN
Are you deaf as well as stupid?
A split-second. BERTIE gapes at him.

BERTIE
What did you say?

BROWN
I said, are you deaf as well as stupid?

BERTIE
Do you know who you address, sir?

BROWN
Whom you address.

BERTIE
The future King!
A beat.

BROWN
Well, everyone's entitled to their opinion.

BERTIE
Out of my way!
Foolishly, BERTIE tries to barge his way past. Suddenly
BROWN loses it completely. He grabs the Prince of Wales by the shoulders and pins
him back, shouting right into his face.

BROWN
LEAVE US ALONE, WHY DON'T YOU!!
For a split-second, BROWN's eyes flicker as he senses he has gone too far. A look of
pure venom in BERTIE'S face, then ...

EXT. WINDSOR CASTLE, QUADRANGLE - NIGHT
Weeks later.
In a roar of hooves and wheels, the Royal Carriage sweeps into the huge quadrangle.
JOHN BROWN stands rigid on the box, glowering at all the world.

CAPTION: "WINDSOR"
INT. WINDSOR CASTLE, SERVANT'S CORRIDOR - NIGHT
A pair of doors open out onto a torchlit driveway as a mass of SERVANTS rush in and
out, ferrying bags an trunks.
BROWN marches in, still charged-up from the strain of the journey's watchfulness. He
spots an UNDER-PORTER snatching a break.

BROWN
You! What's your business here?!

UNDER-PORTER
(jumping to)
Under-porter, sir.

BROWN
Well, don't stand where you shouldn't!
The UNDER-PORTER scrambles up the stairs. A few SERVANTS exchange looks.
BROWN seems more determined than ever to exert his control.

EXT. WINDSOR CASTLE, STABLES - NIGHT
That night.
Carrying an old storm lamp high over his head, BROWN walks towards the stables.

EXT. THE GROUNDS OF WINDSOR CASTLE - DAY
The next day.
BROWN is on horseback, riding with VICTORIA through the grounds. He is still
jumpy, eyes flicking left and right, searching for intruders. They are being followed at
a distance by two EQUERRIES on horseback. VICTORIA frowns peevishly.

VICTORIA
Must they always follow us?

BROWN
I ordered it. It's for your own safety.

VICTORIA
Dear me, you'll be telling me to watch what I eat next.
BROWN doesn't react. A beat.

VICTORIA (CONT'D)
Am I not safe enough with you, John?

BROWN
Aye.
(looking away)
But there are Fenians reported on the mainland.

VICTORIA
(tutting irritably)
The threat from the Irish is greatly exaggerated, I'm sure.

BROWN
(snapping back)
I'll decide when it's exaggerated.
BROWN chucks his horse on, bringing a firm halt to the conversation. A beat. He pulls up suddenly, staring at the shadows in the copse.

VICTORIA
Is anything the matter, John?
(beat)
John?
He stares for along moment and then lets it go.

BROWN
Nothing's the matter.

INT. WINDSOR CASTLE, STABLES - NIGHT
BROWN marches down the line of horse boxes. A stable-lad, BARNEY, is feeding the horses. He looks twitchy.

BROWN
Hey, Barney.

BARNEY
Mr Brown, sir --

BROWN
It's cold out there tonight, Barney.
Reaching his pony, BROWN stops and smiles. The animal lifts its face to him and he softly strokes his muzzle.

BROWN (CONT'D)
Yeah, there's a good girl.
(to Barney)
Have you had a look at this hoof? She was limping badly. I think there might be a stone in it.

BARNEY
Yeah, yeah, I did.

BROWN
Good man. And is she all right?

BARNEY
Yeah.

BROWN
Good. She's a good girl. Aren't you?
Yeah, she's a lovely girl. And you know the Queen's riding tomorrow?

BARNEY
Yeah.

BROWN
(beat)
Are you all right, Barney?
BARNEY twitches again and BROWN realizes too late. The split-second he turns, he sees THREE MEN.

BROWN (CONT'D)
Oh, aye...
The MEN pile onto him and he collapses under their weight.
As he falls, BROWN manages to yank himself round, bang up a fist and fling the others off him. But the FIRST MAN is up again, twisting an arm round his neck and tugging him back.
The others grapple his arms down, but BROWN is incredibly strong. Even now, grunting and scrabbling, he makes them fight to force him back. BARNEY stands transfixed in horror.
Dumping BROWN against the wall, the men step back and start kicking the shit out of him. BROWN curls into a ball, jaw locked, hands over his head. Not a sound.

50

Finally, they back off, panting hard. The FIRST MAN pulls out a bottle of whiskey, yanks back BROWN's head and forces whiskey down his throat. It spills over his face and dribbles down his neck.

INT. WINDSOR CASTLE, QUEEN'S SITTING ROOM - DAY
The next day.
VICTORIA is standing at the windows. The door opens and
LADY ELY walks in.

VICTORIA
Well?

LADY ELY
Mr Brown is unable to attend today.

VICTORIA
Why?

LADY ELY
I believe he is unwell, ma'am.

VICTORIA
Unwell?

LADY ELY
I understand he was in a fight.

VICTORIA
Has he been hurt?

LADY ELY
I believe not, ma'am. I understand -- he'd had rather too much to drink.
VICTORIA walks away and steps behind her desk.

VICTORIA
You may go.
LADY ELY bows and walks out. VICTORIA stares at the desk a moment, then picks up her pen and tries to work. She cannot.

INT. WINDSOR CASTLE, BROWN'S QUARTERS - DAY
BROWN sits on the edge of the bed in only his undergarments. His face, arms, legs and fingers are livid with bruises, but he sits there, stiff-backed and gritting his teeth, while ARCHIE crouches in front of him, tending to his wounds.

BROWN
And she sent no word down?

ARCHIE
They said you were drunk.
(beat)
Why don't you tell her the truth?

BROWN
She'll think it's her fault for keeping me.
ARCHIE completes one of the dressings when BROWN suddenly reaches back and starts trying to put on his shirt.

ARCHIE
What are you doing?!

BROWN
I'm getting dressed.

ARCHIE
You've got three broken ribs, man!

BROWN
I've got my duties to attend to.

ARCHIE
Don't be an idiot! You're in no fit state to go anywhere.

BROWN
She'll be worried about me.

ARCHIE
She'll get over it.

BROWN
I can't let her down now, Archie.

ARCHIE
And when was the last time she put herself out for you? Look, John, whatever she says to you now, in the end you're still a servant.

BROWN
Oh, I'm much more than that.

ARCHIE
Aye, she may say that to you, but the woman can say what she wants.

BROWN

You watch your tongue.

ARCHIE
Come on, man, I'm telling you what you already know.

BROWN
You know nothing about her!

ARCHIE
When are you gonna see it, John? She doesn't give a damn about you.
BROWN lunges for the bedside drawer and pulls out a card showing a coy picture of a pretty woman. He holds it up, eyes blazing.

BROWN
From the Queen!
He reads out the inscription.

BROWN (CONT'D)
My lips may give a message better of
Christmas love than e'en this letter.
(beat)
To my best friend, J.B. from his best friend, V.R.
(he thrusts it in his brother's face)
Best friend!

ARCHIE
Aye.

BROWN
She means it.
ARCHIE stares at him.

ARCHIE
She'll drop you. When she's done with you, she'll drop you.

BROWN
Get out.
(beat)
Out!
ARCHIE steps back but BROWN roars at him.

BROWN (CONT'D)
OUT!!
ARCHIE steps outside and BROWN is left alone.

INT. WINDSOR CASTLE, QUEEN'S SITTING ROOM - DAY

The next day. VICTORIA sits at her desk. PONSONBY hands her letters to sign.

PONSONBY
... to be followed by a visit from
Lady Bridport. She is keen to secure a place for her niece as Maid of
Honor.
VICTORIA signs the last letter and sits back.

VICTORIA
I am tired.
PONSONBY coughs.

PONSONBY
There is one other matter.

VICTORIA
What is it?

PONSONBY
I have a letter, ma'am.

VICTORIA
From whom?

PONSONBY
From Princess Helena and other members of your family.

VICTORIA
(stiffening defensively)
My family is quite capable of communicating with the Queen in person.
PONSONBY does not reply. Finally, VICTORIA is obliged to ask.

VICTORIA (CONT'D)
What do they want?

PONSONBY
They are demanding the dismissal of
John Brown on grounds of drunkeness.
VICTORIA stares through the window, expressionless.

INT. WINDSOR CASTLE, CHAPEL - DAY
VICTORIA walks through the ornate chapel, nervously fingering her handkerchief.
Waiting for her, smiling softly, is the Dean of Windsor, DEAN WELLSELLY.

DEAN WELLSELLY
You wished to see me, ma'am?

She holds his eyes for a moment, then nods.

INT. WINDSOR CASTLE, CHAPEL - DAY

A few minutes later, VICTORIA and DEAN WELLSELLY are seated in a corner of the chapel, talking softly. She cannot bring herself to look at him and so does not notice how carefully he is watching her throughout the interview.

This is incredibly hard for her to say, but she struggles to be as honest as possible.

VICTORIA

My husband tried always to make me think more subtly. Of course he taught me so much and I can never repay my debt to him, or the love I feel, even now. But, in truth, I think I am someone who can only feel things while they are alive to me.

For that reason, I know I do not have a subtle mind. I know that. But I work hard and I try to do my duty.

(she hesitates; she is struggling now)

However, I have noticed of late that my feelings of grief are not so strong and -- that I find myself leaning more upon the comfort of living friends.

(beat)

Friends close to me now.

She stops herself. She is crying. DEAN WELLSELLY watches her a moment, then speaks close, choosing his words carefully.

DEAN WELLSELLY

Your Majesty, a settled resignation is more lasting proof of affection than active grief. If the good Lord sees fit to bring one into contact with congenial fellow beings, one should not analyze one's reaction too deeply.

To allow oneself to be comforted by someone else need not imply any disloyalty to the memory of the loved one.

Silence. VICTORIA stares into the long, dark chapel.

Gradually, as she takes in the tone of his remarks, her disappointment turns to anger.

INT. WINDSOR CASTLE, QUEEN'S SITTING ROOM - DAY

The next day, VICTORIA stands at the far window and her back to the room. Lined up against the wall are BERTIE and his siblings.

VICTORIA

Sir Henry.

PONSONBY steps forward.

PONSONBY

Ma'am?

VICTORIA

Please tell the Princess, and other signatories to this letter, that the Queen will not be dictated to, or made to alter, in any way, what she has found to answer for her comfort.

(beat)
Do I make myself clear?

PONSONBY
Ma'am.
A beat.

VICTORIA
You may go.
They all file out.

EXT. THE GROUNDS OF WINDSOR CASTLE - DAY
A few days later.
BROWN and VICTORIA are riding on horseback. Although better than he was,
BROWN'S face is still badly bruised.
They turn a corner banked by trees. BROWN is watching the
QUEEN closely. She stops.

VICTORIA
I would like to get down.
Without a word, BROWN dismounts and helps her off her horse.

VICTORIA (CONT'D)
John?

BROWN
Yes, ma'am?

VICTORIA
I was told you were in a fight.

BROWN
Yes, ma'am.

VICTORIA
Has someone seen to those bruises?

BROWN
Yes, ma'am.
A beat.

BROWN (CONT'D)
Ma'am?

VICTORIA
Yes?

BROWN

Having considered my position here at court, I have come to the conclusion that it is in the best interest of
Your Majesty that I should resign.

VICTORIA

I do not accept.
A beat.

BROWN

I had foreseen that you would not.
But Your Majesty should understand -- that my mind will not be changed in this. I leave for Deeside --

VICTORIA

(cutting in)
The Queen forbids it.
(beat)
I cannot allow it because I cannot live without you. Without you, I cannot find the strength to be who I must be. Please.
She takes his hand to her mouth and kisses it gently, then looks at him, utterly helpless.

VICTORIA (CONT'D)

Promise me you won't let them send me back.
A long silence. BROWN holds her hand tight.

BROWN

I promise.

FADE TO BLACK.
CAPTION: "1868"
FADE IN:
EXT. LOWLANDS - DAY
A few weeks later.
A tiny horse-drawn carriage creeps across a huge Highland landscape.

DISRAELI (V.O.)

Yesterday, Gladstone talked for three hours on the Irish Church Bill ... I am as guilty as the rest of underestimating his reforming zeal.
Tory days may be numbered, but I fancy there yet remains one last hope of deliverance.
Wheresoever the blame lies, we must now close ranks and defend Mrs Brown's England.
As for my interminable journey to the land of
Calvin, oatcakes and sulphur ...

EXT. BALMORAL CASTLE - DAY

DISRAELI hurries through the pouring rain.

DISRAELI (O.S.)
... no Prime Minister made greater sacrifice than attempting to run the country six hundred miles north of civilization.
Reaching the castle, he hurries inside and the great doors bang behind him.

INT. BALMORAL CASTLE, QUEEN'S DRAWING ROOM - DAY
The next day.
QUEEN VICTORIA is playing the piano like she walks, with great vim and vigor. The tune is some quaint Scottish ballad which she belts out in her clear strong voice, almost drowning out PRINCE ARTHUR, PRINCE LOUISE and PRINCE
LEOPOLD who are meant to be accompanying her. They stand in a nervous semi-circle, fumbling their harmonies.
Ignoring them completely, VICTORIA bobs up her head with a quizzical smile to make sure she is being appreciated.
DISRAELI and the rest of the HOUSEHOLD stand a few yards off, smiling rigidly. DISRAELI, the consummate politician to his inch-high insteps, out-smiles the lot of them. This man is in raptures of delight. And the more liquid his smiles, the happier he makes VICTORIA. He beams, she belts, until her children are drowned out completely.
And then, with characteristic suddenness, VICTORIA stops playing and launches into one of her tirades. The
HOUSEHOLD wobbles in shock like children on a switch-back, but DISRAELI glides smoothly from delight to sober concern.

VICTORIA
How dare the Irish break with the
Anglicans?
If Albert were alive today he would never allow the Crown to give up
Church patronage. No, the Irish must be told, very firmly, to stay exactly where they are. It is the thin edge of the wedge, Mr Disraeli. Next, you will be telling me that the Crown no longer governs this nation.
A beat. A nervous silence in the Household.

DISRAELI
Your Majesty remains at the very epicenter of governance. As for your people, look no further than the sales of your Highland Journals to see in what affection the nation holds their
Queen.
(beat)
You sell even more copies than Mr
Dickens.

VICTORIA
But I lack your prose, Mr Disraeli.

VICTORIA gives him a tiny smile. DISRAELI acknowledges it, then steers the conversation back.

DISRAELI
Of course I understand your concern.
You miss your people.
(a pause)
And they miss you.
VICTORIA registers a slight flicker of defensiveness at the implied criticism.

VICTORIA
Then they may read about me.

DISRAELI
Indeed, and for that they are eternally grateful.

VICTORIA
Is that not enough?

DISRAELI
In so many ways ... and yet it is your presence they crave. A figurehead.
VICTORIA has the measure of him.

VICTORIA
I never thought to be bullied by you,
Mr Disraeli. You, I thought, understood a widow's grief.

DISRAELI
Forgive me, ma'am, I cannot speak for the nation, only for myself. As Prime
Minister I confess I miss your presence, but that is only an expression of my own selfish
desires and I should not burden you with it.
The Household waits. Has he clawed himself back? VICTORIA acknowledges his
apology. Her voice drops and she talks directly to DISRAELI, straight from the heart.

VICTORIA
I stay here because I am happy.
(beat)
Is that such a terrible crime?

DISRAELI
No, ma'am.
At this moment the far door opens and BROWN walks in.

BROWN
Time for your walk.

Without a word, VICTORIA rises from her chair and starts following him out. As they pass DISRAELI, she stops.

VICTORIA
This is my good John Brown.

DISRAELI
(taking him in)
Yes.

VICTORIA
I have asked him to show you a little of Highland life while you are with us at Balmoral.
BROWN measures DISRAELI suspiciously.

BROWN
What brings you here?

DISRAELI
A man can refuse only so many invitations from his Queen. It was remiss of me not to come earlier.
VICTORIA smiles. BROWN stares.

BROWN
What do you know about the Highlands?

DISRAELI
I am a blank sheet.

BROWN
Do you hunt?

DISRAELI
Occasionally.

BROWN
Dare say you can be taught.

DISRAELI
To shoot perhaps, but not to kill.

BROWN
If you hunt, you kill.
DISRAELI counters effortlessly.

DISRAELI
Well then, I'll do my best.

EXT. HIGHLANDS, GLEN GELDER - DAY

Staying close to the ground we develop through a series of shots showing the other highlands -- sheet rain against heather and gorse, rivulets of water slashing through mud, crude pathways sliding in wind and all ball-breakingly cold.

Coming up the hill, we begin to make out a hunting party.

The sound first. Like a small army, crashing their way up the winding path. GHILLIES urging on their horses and dogs, guns and equipment jangling off pony-hacks an then the tall figure of JOHN BROWN striding out in front.

Making no concession to anyone, he force-marches them up the hill, eyes on the hunt ahead. Behind them trot the men on horseback -- DISRAELI, PONSONBY, BERTIE and other

GENTLEMEN, each led by GHILLIES and ATTENDANTS, among them

ARCHIE.

Suddenly, BROWN stops and raises a hand. The party halts.

He listens for a second. Satisfied that he has found his quarry, he brings his hand down and the party of gentlemen dismount as quietly as they can.

As he waits, BROWN winces slightly from the pain in his side. He pulls a flask of whiskey from his sporran and drinks. All the time, DISRAELI keeps his eyes on BROWN.

EXT. HIGHLANDS, GLEN GELDER - DAY

The stalking.

Everyone is now fanned out along the hillside, a ghillie to each gentleman, slowly and silently moving up the hill.

DISRAELI stalks with BROWN, panting hard to keep up, eyes on his man, trying to make no sound.

Suddenly, BROWN stops. Very slowly he rises. DISRAELI rides alongside and sees ...

A huge stag staring majestically across the hillside.

Keeping his movements smooth and slow, BROWN brings up his rifle, cocks it and offers DISRAELI the kill. With a deferential gesture of the hands, DISRAELI declines. BROWN stares at him a split-second, raises the rifle to his shoulder and fires.

EXT. HIGHLANDS, GLEN GELDER - DAY

The kill.

A rapid montage of guns firing, as we cut to ...

INT. BALMORAL CASTLE - DAY

BROWN sweeps in from the hunt, DISRAELI dripping at his side.

BROWN

(demonstrating with his rifle)

Always remember, you keep it tight to your shoulder, you absorb the kick.

Aim for the head. Then imagine it's

Gladstone.

DISRAELI
(smiling)
Quite.
BROWN pulls out his flask and offers some to DISRAELI, who declines. He watches BROWN take a long swig.

INT. BALMORAL CASTLE, UPPER SERVANT'S TABLE - NIGHT
That night.
BROWN is standing at his place, drinking steadily. He has a sheet of paper and a pen and is ticking off a list.
Lined up in front of him, trying desperately not to laugh, are five or six UPPER SERVANTS including the pretty
ASSISTANT DRESSER and BERTIE'S VALET. They each step up, one at a time, to make their report.

BROWN
(ticking as he goes)
... Back doors, West Wing.

UPPER SERVANT 1
Checked and locked, sir.

BROWN
Side doors, East Wing.

ASSISTANT DRESSER
Checked and locked, sir.

BROWN
Louder, girl!

ASSISTANT DRESSER
(creasing up)
Checked and locked, sir.

BROWN
Kitchen and lower house.

BERTIE'S VALET
Checked and locked, sir.

BROWN
Back and upper corridors.

UPPER SERVANT 2
Checked and locked, sir.

BROWN
Front door.
(beat)
Checked and locked.
Folding up the paper, BROWN downs his glass of whiskey and sits. On his nod, dinner is served by UNDER SERVANTS amid a clatter of cutlery and chat.
ARCHIE looks across at his brother but BROWN is hunched over his plate, pecking at his food.
Someone titters and ARCHIE looks up. BERTIE'S VALET coughs. BROWN slowly lifts his head. His eyes have the slightly unfocused look of too much drink. It is clear to
ARCHIE that he is about to be sent-up.

BERTIE'S VALET
(with a smug smile)
Did you see any Irish assassins today,
Mr Brown?
Brown doesn't react.

BERTIE'S VALET (CONT'D)
We heard the dogs were Fenian sympathizers.
Brown drinks.

BERTIE'S VALET (CONT'D)
Or was it the stag ...?
Everyone bursts out laughing. Brown slams down his glass.

BROWN
There's not a soul here cares about that wee woman's safety except me!
She'd die in a ditch if I wasn't there to look out for her --
He stops. ARCHIE has come across to his brother's chair and pulls gently on his arm.
BROWN stares at the SERVANTS. Everyone is about to burst out laughing. Keeping his dignity, he pushes back his chair and lets ARCHIE lead him away.
As BROWN reaches the double doors, the laughter hits him in the back like a wave. ARCHIE holds him steady.

INT. BALMORAL CASTLE, BROWN'S QUARTERS - NIGHT
BROWN is lying on a grubby bed. ARCHIE is looking around the untidy room. For the first time, he notices a thick manuscript on the table. BROWN follows his eyes.

ARCHIE
What's this?

BROWN
It's a diary.

ARCHIE
Be careful who sees it.

BROWN
What do you take me for?
ARCHIE turns back to BROWN.

ARCHIE
You should have someone look after you.

BROWN
I'm all right. I just need to rest up a wee bit.
(feeling everything spin)
The room ... You don't have to stay.
BROWN shuts his eyes and starts to drift. ARCHIE watches over him.

ARCHIE
The place is a mess.

BROWN
I can't move to tidy.

ARCHIE
It's what the maids are for.

BROWN
I'm not having some prattler going through my things.
A beat.

ARCHIE
Won't you give yourself a rest, John?
She's other people to look out for her.

BROWN
She needs me, Archie. She canna do without me, she said it to my face.
(his hands come up to cover his eyes)
How can I stop now?

INT. BALMORAL CASTLE, SERVANT'S CORRIDOR - DAY
Dawn the next morning.
BROWN is scrambling into his jacket as he hurries down the stairs.

EXT. BALMORAL CASTLE - DAY

BROWN crashes out of a side-door -- just fully dressed -- to be met by the smiling figure of DISRAELI. He is got up in smart walking boots, plus-fours and a tweed jacket.

BROWN
You sent for me.

DISRAELI
I've been called back to London. My last day. I thought I might take a walk on Lochnagar.
BROWN stares straight back.

EXT. LOCHNAGER - DAY
An hour later, BROWN leads DISRAELI up the hill. BROWN has his head down, on with the job. DISRAELI slows to a halt.

DISRAELI
Princes and Lords are but the breath of kings, An honest man's the noblest work of God.
(beat)
You must miss such magnificent views.

BROWN
I don't think about it.
They reach the top and continue along the high ground.
DISRAELI glances at BROWN and notices the limp.

DISRAELI
Forgive me, I've called you out and you should have been resting.

BROWN
I'm fine.

DISRAELI
You're injured.

BROWN
It's nothing.

DISRAELI
Still, someone must attend you. Your wife should not have let you out.

BROWN
I'm not married.

DISRAELI
(deadpan)

Oh.

BROWN
This is the top.
DISRAELI admires the view for a moment, then continues.

DISRAELI
I confess, I sometimes feel as if I am not married myself, I see my wife so little. But I'm forgetting the rewards.
He looks across. BROWN keeps staring ahead.

DISRAELI (CONT'D)
The look on their faces when one walks into the room. Still gives one a ridiculous thrill.

BROWN
I wouldn't know.

DISRAELI
Surely --

BROWN
(interrupts)
What I do, I do for my Queen.

DISRAELI
Was there never ambition?

BROWN
(beat)
Maybe, once.

DISRAELI
Then I envy yo.

BROWN
Why?

DISRAELI
To have achieved one's ambition, or to have reconciled oneself to its limits, is a lifetime's work.

BROWN
I do what I do.

DISRAELI
For Her Majesty.

BROWN
Aye.

DISRAELI
But yourself?
(beat)
What about John Brown?

BROWN
I said.
(beat)
I serve the Queen.

DISRAELI
No other aspiration?
BROWN stares for a long moment. Finally he speaks.

BROWN
To see her safe.
DISRAELI steps a little closer.

DISRAELI
You will not be unaware of the threat now posed by Republicanism.

BROWN
Why do you think I keep her here?

DISRAELI
Ah, but therein lies the paradox. It is her very isolation that encourages the malcontents.
The longer she is away, the stronger they become; and who, honestly, can promise
security against that? However many doors you lock, someone will always get in.
Even here.
BROWN watches him, eyes alert.

BROWN
So...?

DISRAELI
The truth is, the Queen would be safer doing her duty and returning south to her public.
John Bull loves her and
John Bull is her best defense.

BROWN
Her mind is set. She won't change now.

DISRAELI
She trusts you, John.
DISRAELI is right on his shoulder now, like his own voice.

BROWN
They don't see it.

DISRAELI
See what?

BROWN
The threat.
(beat)
I tell them, but they don't see it.

DISRAELI
They aren't as watchful as you.

BROWN
Too busy looking after themselves.

DISRAELI
The greasy pole.

BROWN
No loyalty.

DISRAELI
No love.
Silence. For a moment BROWN seems unaware that someone else has said that.

BROWN
I promised to protect her from people like you.

DISRAELI
For once in my life, I am not the issue.

BROWN
She'll never understand it.

DISRAELI
In time, she will.

BROWN
She'll think I betrayed her.

DISRAELI
But others will know that you acted for the greater good.
BROWN stares off into the distance.

EXT. LOCH MUICK - DAY
The next day.
BROWN is rowing VICTORIA across the loch. The EQUERRIES wait on the shore.
VICTORIA trails her hand in the water, frowning at the surface. BROWN concentrates
on the oars, slipping them carefully through the water.

VICTORIA
I received a letter today from Mr
Disraeli. Parliament is calling for my return to public duties.
(beat)
Why won't they let us be?
BROWN does not answer.

VICTORIA (CONT'D)
He insists that the country expects me to preside over the opening of the new session. I
refuse to offer sustenance to enable his weakening grip.
Besides, you know how much I should hate it. It frightens me.
She notices that BROWN has said nothing.

VICTORIA (CONT'D)
John?
BROWN does not look at her. Finally:

BROWN
We can't always have what we wish.
VICTORIA stares at him.

INT. BALMORAL CASTLE, QUEEN'S DRAWING ROOM - DAY
Later that day.
VICTORIA and BROWN are in the middle of a blazing row in front of the entire
Household, including PONSONBY, JENNER and LADY ELY.

VICTORIA
Duty?! You talk about duty?!

BROWN
If duty and safety are served by the same end then, aye, I do.

VICTORIA
I cannot believe you are saying this?
You, who I have relied on all this time --

BROWN
(cutting in)
Have I ever let you down before--?

VICTORIA
(as if he had not spoken)
-- You stand there and tell me it is my duty ... after all you promised me!

BROWN
I'm breaking no promises!

VICTORIA
You are forcing me to do the very thing you know I fear most!

BROWN
For god's sake, woman, I'm just trying to keep you safe!

VICTORIA
I will not hear any more about my safety!! You made me a promise and now you have broken it!
BROWN rounds on her, deeply wounded.

BROWN
-- When I took you out riding, come rain or shine, because I knew it was right for you, when I kept the bairns off your back so you could have a bit of peace, when I saw you safe from home to home and you didn't even know
I was there...! All I've ever thought about is you!

VICTORIA
Then why send me back to them?!

BROWN
Because I have to!
(pause
Will you no listen to me, woman?
Face turned from him, VICTORIA replies in a brittle voice.

VICTORIA
Do not presume to talk to your Queen in that manner.
A long silence. BROWN watches her, but she will not look at him again. Finally, she walks very slowly across the room. She turns in the doorway, her voice faltering slightly.

VICTORIA (CONT'D)
Doctor Jenner, I feel unwell. I shall retire to my chamber. Please attend me presently.
As the door slams, we ...

FADE TO BLACK.
CAPTION: "NOVEMBER"
FADE IN:
INT. BALMORAL CASTLE, DINING ROOM - DAY
A few weeks later.

Close on a door as it opens. The ROYAL FAMILY are eating lunch with members of the UPPER HOUSEHOLD. VICTORIA walks in with LADY ELY.

A great scraping of chairs as everyone drops their forks and stands. Clearly, they were not expecting her. In silence, VICTORIA steps up and takes her place at the head of the table.

At last, PONSONBY leans forward deferentially.

PONSONBY
May I say, how glad I am to see Your
Majesty so much recovered.
VICTORIA nods, then turns and looks about at the others.
PRINCESS ALEXANDRA is seated at the far end of the table.
VICTORIA frowns.

VICTORIA
Where is my son?

PRINCESS ALEXANDRA
Prince Albert is at Windsor, ma'am.

VICTORIA
Why is he not here?

PRINCESS ALEXANDRA
He is sick, ma'am.

VICTORIA
Then why are you not with him?

PRINCESS ALEXANDRA
You ordered all members of the Royal
Family to attend you at Balmoral.

VICTORIA
What is the matter with him?

PRINCESS ALEXANDRA
He has typhoid fever, ma'am.
VICTORIA stares blankly at DOCTOR JENNER.

VICTORIA
No. You are mistaken. Prince Albert, my husband, had typhoid fever. I asked what was wrong with my son.

JENNER
The same, your Majesty.
VICTORIA stops. She stares down the length of the table.
A long pause.

VICTORIA
Why was I not informed?

JENNER
I did not consider it wise, in the circumstances, to tax your nerves.

VICTORIA
How ill is he?
No answer.

VICTORIA (CONT'D)
(to Alexandra)
Alex?

VICTORIA (CONT'D)
He is not well, ma'am.
A beat.

VICTORIA (CONT'D)
I must go to him.
Suddenly, VICTORIA stands. Chairs bang back as everyone leaps to their feet.

VICTORIA (CONT'D)
We must leave at once.
Abruptly, VICTORIA turns for the door and the room erupts into activity.

INT. BALMORAL CASTLE, CORRIDOR - DAY
BROWN stands in the corridor, a little nonplussed by the servants and Householders hurrying about in every direction.

EXT. BALMORAL CASTLE - DAY
Half an hour later, BROWN races up to the Queen's carriage amid a swarm of servants, ladies' maids and Householders rushing to be ready in time.
Suddenly the huge castle doors open and VICTORIA bustles out with her entourage in tow. BROWN -- only just in time
- yanks open the door for VICTORIA to step past him and take her place. She ignores him completely.

BROWN slams the doors. As he looks up, he sees his brother
ARCHIE staring at him from across the courtyard. For a second the two brothers hold
each other's gaze. It's obvious that ARCHIE has noticed the Queen's indifference.
BROWN turns away and mounts the box as the carriage races away under him.

INT. WINDSOR CASTLE, PRINCE'S BEDCHAMBER - DAY
Some days later. A tableau.
QUEEN VICTORIA sits at the foot of the bed, a matriarch surrounded by her ROYAL
FAMILY. They watch DOCTOR JENNER bend to examine the ghostly figure of
BERTIE. He listens for a pulse. Finally, he looks up.

JENNER
Better.
VICTORIA lets out a deep breath. She takes hold of
PRINCESS ALEXANDRA'S hand.

VICTORIA
Should the good Lord see fit to spare my son, I will order a mass to be celebrated at St.
George's. The people must share with their Queen, her prayers and hopes for their
future
King.

INT. WINDSOR CASTLE, CORRIDOR OUTSIDE BEDCHAMBER - DAY
A few minutes later, BROWN stands in the corridor when the door bursts open and
VICTORIA marches straight past him with PONSONBY at her side.

PONSONBY
(aside to BROWN)
The Queen will be riding to St.
George's on the fifth.

BROWN
(launching straight in)
I recommend Her Majesty uses the covered carriage with a full Horse
Guard. In the event of any disturbance I will ensure --

VICTORIA
(cutting in)
I will ride to St. George's in an open carriage. It is time the Queen was seen by her
public.
VICTORIA turns and disappears down the corridor, followed by PONSONBY. We
linger on BROWN'S humiliation, closer and closer until ...

EXT. WINDSOR CASTLE, ST. GEORGE'S - DAY
Some weeks later.

A series of angles on BROWN as he walks amid the mass of onlookers pressing against a cordon of guards surrounding the cathedral. All the time, his eyes flick left and right, searching the faces in front of him for potential assassins. Over his intense watchfulness we hear ...

DEAN WELLSELLY (O.S.)
... praise and magnify thy glorious name for that thou has raised thy servant Albert Edward, Prince of Wales from the bed of sickness.
We pray thee to perfect the recovery of thy servant and to crown him day by day with more abundant blessings both for body and soul, through Jesus
Christ our Lord ...
The CONGREGATION mutters a vast ...

CONGREGATION (O.S.)
Amen.

EXT. WINDSOR CASTLE, ST. GEORGE'S - DAY
VICTORIA and other members of the ROYAL FAMILY walk down the steps towards the cheering crowd. As DEAN WELLSELLY and BROWN follow, BROWN sees ARTHUR O'CONNER break from the onlookers, pulling out a gun. BROWN yells out:

BROWN
NO!!
He races toward O'CONNER and hits him flying, bangs him to the ground and twists the gun out of his hand. As they fall we hear laughter and:

BERTIE (O.S.)
So there he is, Arthur O'Conner...

INT. WINDSOR CASTLE, DINING HALL - NIGHT
It's a few days later and BERTIE is entertaining a private dinner party. They include QUEEN VICTORIA, PRINCESS
ALEXANDRA, PRINCESS LOUISE and HENRY PONSONBY. BROWN is in attendance. He stands off to one side, near the door.

BERTIE
(bristling with confidence)
... all seven stone of the man, paddling madly towards us through a sea of Horse Guards, waving something that looks vaguely like a pen. I thought he must be one of the mother's ardent readership in search of the
Royal indenture...
More chortling. VICTORIA watches her son, smiling proudly.
BROWN looks straight ahead.

BERTIE (CONT'D)

I believe I saw him first and then alerted Brown. I'm not convinced that he wasn't taking a snooze on top of the box. Anyway, we had our man pinned down and I must say, Brown acquitted himself admirably. Of course the gun was a fake, but all the same, it was well done.

No-one registers BROWN. But while VICTORIA does not look at him, she is acutely aware of his presence.

VICTORIA
I intend Brown to be rewarded with a special medal cast in gold. It will be called The Devoted Service Medal.

The guests applaud politely. BERTIE clinks his glass for attention and raises it high.

BERTIE
A toast. Victoria Regina!

The others raise their glasses in unison.

EVERYONE
Victoria Regina!

VICTORIA smiles. BROWN remains alone by the door.

DISRAELI (O.S.)
The people of England have expressed in a manner which cannot be mistaken, that they will uphold the ancient monarchy of England ...

INT. CRYSTAL PALACE - DAY
DISRAELI is delivering his come-back speech at a banquet of
Tory delegates.

DISRAELI
... If the first great object of the
Tory Party is to maintain the institutions of the country, the second is, in my opinion, to maintain the Empire of England ... the hereditary, the traditionary policy of the Tory Party. Go to your homes, teach them these truths, which will soon be imprinted on the conscience of the land ...

FADE TO BLACK.
CAPTION: "1883"
FADE IN:
INT. WINDSOR CASTLE, BROWN'S QUARTERS - NIGHT
The sound of rain driven hard against a window. We creep slowly down the corridor until we are back with the fifty year-old BROWN. With his whiskey for company, he is sitting at his desk, writing in the diary.

The diary-manuscript is now falling apart with wear, but there remain a few blank pages. Slowly, he fills them in.

BROWN (V.O.)

We should not live in expectation of contentment. Fifteen years of vigilance will not guarantee peace of mind. Yesterday, intruders were again reported in the South Wing. I believe my prompt arrival may have averted any crisis, but it was a timely reminder. It is a great comfort to me that my efforts in securing the Queen's safety over the years have not been in vain.

Certainly Her Majesty sends me no word that she's dissatisfied. And I feel sure that if she were unhappy she would have found the occasion to speak to me in person, as she has so often done in the past.

A knock at the door.

BROWN (CONT'D)
What is it?
We hear a young PAGE, breathless from running.

PAGE
North woods, sir.
BROWN grabs his gun and rushes out.

EXT. WINDSOR CASTLE, QUADRANGLE - NIGHT
BROWN appears at the door and strides into the storm. He walks quickly across the wide quadrangle, rain soaking his hair and clothes.
Two GUARDS watch BROWN as he races out into the storm.
A coin flips through the air to be caught by an outstretched hand. The second GUARD grins.

EXT. THE GROUNDS OF WINDSOR CASTLE - NIGHT
BROWN races across the open ground towards the forest.

EXT. THE GROUNDS OF WINDSOR CASTLE, FOREST - NIGHT
And now we are back with the opening sequence. Truncated, severe, and shot from a slightly different angle. The driving rain, BROWN hurtling through the trees, the crack to his left, he spins and plunges on.

EXT. THE GROUNDS OF WINDSOR CASTLE, FOREST - NIGHT
Close-up on BROWN as he bangs against a tree, heaving for air. He searches the dark, stops, listens and races on.

EXT. THE GROUNDS OF WINDSOR CASTLE, FOREST - NIGHT
BROWN tears through the trees, pistol raised at full arm's length.

EXT. THE GROUNDS OF WINDSOR CASTLE, FOREST - NIGHT
He bursts into a clearing, breaks to the centre and stops.
Pistol raised, he turns a circle, eyes on the wildly swaying trees. A branch snaps behind him. He spins round, bellows deep from his heart:

BROWN

God save the Queen!!
And fires.

INT. WINDSOR CASTLE, CORRIDOR - NIGHT
A few days later.
VICTORIA is moving swiftly down a long corridor with LADY
ELY. They arrive at a door. VICTORIA stands facing it.

VICTORIA
(quietly)
How long has he been this sick?

LADY ELY
A few days, ma'am.

VICTORIA
Why was I not told earlier?
LADY ELY doesn't answer. VICTORIA knows anyway. She nods.
LADY ELY knocks. The door is opened by a young UNDER
SERVANT who gawps at the sight of Her Majesty standing here in the servant's
quarters. VICTORIA walks in.

INT. WINDSOR CASTLE, BROWN'S QUARTERS - NIGHT
The room has been cleared of bottles, but the thinness of the life here shocks her deeply.
The cheap furniture, the anonymous prints, the bed and, finally, the sight of BROWN.
He is lying in bed, barely conscious. After a moment, he opens his eyes and stares at
her. She steps forward, smiling nervously.
Her voice is the old voice, between friends.

VICTORIA
You should never have gone out in such foul weather.

BROWN
Someone has to look after you.
(pause)
It could've been someone. It was before.

VICTORIA
Yes. Yes it was.
He cannot speak. It's difficult for her too, but she speaks for him.

VICTORIA (CONT'D)
My Ministers are as impertinent as ever. Dispatches are now so numerous, they come
in a trunk. Sometimes I do believe they will never stop. Endless letters...
Her voice falters. A pause

VICTORIA (CONT'D)
I know I have not always been the loyal friend you deserved, John. And yet here I am now, even now, feeling desperate at the thought of losing you.
She starts to cry.

BROWN
Don't be silly, woman.
His old, familiar gruffness makes her smile and she pulls herself together. Seeing a bowl of water on the side table, she steps across. Carefully folding a cloth in four, she rinses it in the water and gently wipes his face.
Leaning closer, she is about to touch his face when BROWN gestures protectively.

BROWN (CONT'D)
Not too near.

INT. WINDSOR CASTLE, CORRIDOR - DAY
A week later. PONSONBY and JENNER stand at the window overlooking the grounds.

JENNER
Erysipelas.

PONSONBY
Not too protracted, I hope.

JENNER
(shakes his head)
A few days...
(beat)
When he heard, the Prince of Wales threw the bust from the window of the Royal Gallery. It took four hours to gather the fragments.
A beat.

PONSONBY
The Queen wishes to publish an account of him.

JENNER
Dear oh dear.

PONSONBY
We think she can be dissuaded.
(beat)
Have you had a glance at the diary?

JENNER
Yes.

PONSONBY
Quite.
(beat)
I think I'd best take it back.

JENNER
Of course.
He brings out BROWN'S tatty diary-manuscript and hands it over to PONSONBY. The two men move away from the window, to go their separate ways. Daily business beckons.

JENNER (CONT'D)
Where did you find it by the way?

PONSONBY
Some young page was boasting about having seen it.
(beat)
Lucky.
JENNER nods.

JENNER
Well, no rest for the wicked, Henry.

PONSONBY
No, indeed.
The two men head off in opposite directions down the corridor.

Printed in Great Britain
by Amazon